LEAPS AND BOUNDARIES

PSYCHOANALYSIS REVISITED

DORIS TREISMAN

Edited by Susan A. Gordon

OCEANIDES PRESS

Published by Oceanides Press
737 Calhoun Street, Port Townsend, Washington 98368

Printed in the United States of America

Photo on Page 1 by H. Brownell Chalstrom III,
taken in Schwäbisch Hall, West Germany, 1988.

Photo on Page 47 by H. Kubach,
from the book *Schwäbisch Hall, liebenswert und voller Leben,*
by H. Kubach and von Willi Eller,
verlag Oscar Mahl KG, Schwäbisch Hall, 1981.

Photo on Page 75 by Doris Treisman,
taken in the garden of the Rosenbourg Castle in Copenhagen, Denmark.

Leaps and Boundaries

by Doris Treisman

ACKNOWLEDGEMENTS

Many thanks to the men and women who shared their metaphors, aphorisms, images and dreams as they explored their memories and associations within the scope of psychotherapy.

Special thanks to Sigmund Freud and Carl Jung who provided us with excellent techniques for probing our inner worlds, thereby enabling each of us to recognize our incestuous wishes, our oedipal fears, our narcissistic injuries, our shadows, and our transformations.

CONTENTS

The therapist's voice appears in *italic type,* the patient's voice is in "book" type.

Leaps and Boundaries

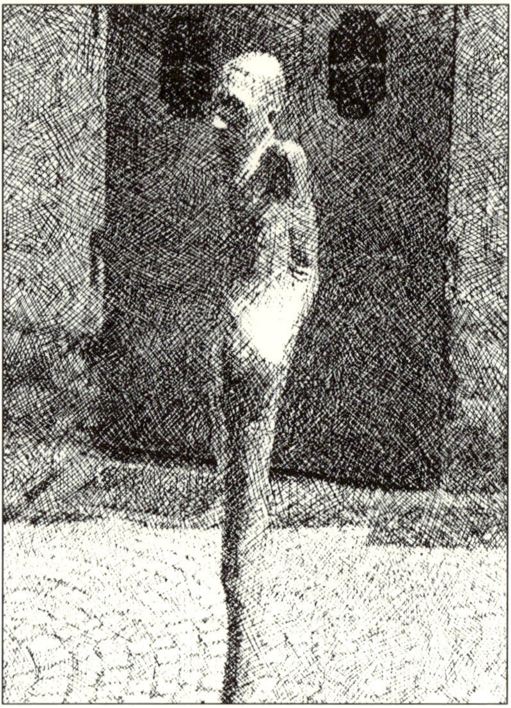

I resurrect my fear
And redirect my anger
Over and over and over again.

BOOK I

PROEM

TESTAMENT

Mothers and fathers
Beget
Anxious, prejudiced children
Eager, intelligent children
Depressed, borderline children
Talented, industrious children
Addicts, groupies
Street people, scientists and artists.

Eager, talented, anxious, depressed
Children
Become the adults
Who may or may not
Beget.

CONNECTION, SEPARATION, AND RECONNECTION, AD INFINITUM

We leave infancy many times in the course of our lives and we carry both pleasant and unpleasant memories of the separations. It is not always easy to see the ways in which we substitute others for Mother and Father and all they represent, how we negotiate feeding our needs under the guise of friendship, generosity, love and righteous indignation, how we blame others for our developmental detours and dead ends, how we credit others for our pleasures and accomplishments, or how we avenge our early hurts in subtle and not so subtle ways.

In our selective memories, both conscious and unconscious, we find many clues to typical and atypical development. Uncovering memories in order to lay the unpleasant feelings to rest is what psychotherapy is about.

In the following pages I try to describe the development of the therapeutic alliance, the spiral motion of learning, and the ultimate readiness for deeper exploration.

CHAPTER I

THE ALLIANCE BEGINS

Tell me your about your family,
The one into which you were born.
What kind of life have you made for yourself?
What kind of life would you like?

TREASURE HUNT

In memory there are buried truths.
In memory there are buried lies.
In memory there are buried thorns that fester.

Aching hearts and creaking joints
May well result from festering thorns
And partial truths that need to be examined.

To disinter the festering thorns
And rearrange the truths and lies
Mix therapy with salty, sanguine humor.

Then, perhaps, you'll find the trust,
The kind of trust that triggers change,
The kind of change that comes from healing wounds.

HISTORY

I was a naturally friendly child
With an exuberance for life.

I was molded by disappointments
Through awkward adolescence
To stubborn adult.

The very early milk I drank
Was flavored with depression,
The milk itself was rich with love,
And hope for humankind.

I have loved many lovers,
Lost numerous pounds,
Bought varied toys,
Tried some drugs.

The dissatisfactions that churn beneath my surface
Simmer and boil, but can no longer be ignored.

PROCESS

Look at your feelings.
Look at your memories.
Look at your symptoms.
Look at your boundaries.

Don't be afraid of them.
Don't be ashamed of them.
Don't be proud of them.

Let us just look at them,
Together.

After you see them clearly,
You may bury them or parade them,
Depending on your style.

But first, let us look at them,
Clearly.

BREAKING THE CYCLE

My grandfather was ill tempered
My mother was depressed.
I am afraid to look clearly at myself.

I avert my gaze.
Into my peripheral vision come glimpses
Of me the child, me the baby, me the infant.

And you ask
If I feel loved.

I answer, "Yes,
I feel loved enough
To do my share of the work
Of repairing the structure of my life."

RECIPE FOR AN ANALYTIC SOLUTION

Objective: To disinter the festering thorns.

Lie quietly on your analyst's couch
And listen to your voices.
Let them tell your story
Without your conscious control.

Heed the conversations that ensue
Between the many voices in your head
And the many voices of your analyst.

After your story is told,
And analyzed,
And understood,
Allow your ego
To supervise your id.

RECIPE FOR A CHEMICAL SOLUTION

Objective: To rearrange the truth and lies.

Find the early rage
That binds to the present anger.
Cool down the early rage.

Find the early warmth
That binds to the present love.
Heat up the early warmth.

Find the early fear
That cements the present anger.
Look at the fear, clearly.

Stir in your solution
To dissolve the crazyglue
With which you built your structure.

Then, develop your life
With love, learning, hope
Warmth, and respect.

CHAPTER 2

SPIRAL MOTION

During which
trust and autonomy,
warmth and anger
grow new dimensions
that allow further development
of the therapeutic alliance.

THE SPIRAL

Round and round I go
In an ever widening circle.
Then I narrow down the focus
Before I zero in.

SOS

When rage runs deep
My dreams frighten me.
My reasonable, logical self
Hibernates.

I subdue my creative spirit.
I plod wearily through my responsibilities,
Blaming and attacking everyone,
Including myself.

I look for magic,
Magic that will somehow
Decrease my rage, change my world.

ANXIETY

I'm human, I'm frightened,
I'm angry, and I'm in love.

My heart pounds
My stomach churns,
My sphincters tighten,
My spine rigidifies.

Adrenaline flows
To ready me for action.

Tears also flow
To wash away the hurt
Of helplessness,

And my libido keeps trying to find
A way to love and be loved.

PRISONERS

When we feel loved
We interpret life
With charity and kindness.

When we feel unloved,
We interpret life
From an infant's perspective,
With a baby's rage.
And we reject friendliness
From any direction.

FEAR AND ANGER

Sometimes my anger wakes me up,
And sometimes it puts me to sleep.
Sometimes their anger frightened me,
And sometimes it woke me up.

The landscapes I see when I'm awake
Don't resemble my dreams or nightmares.

Is it anger that imprisons you
Or is it fear of anger
That holds you fast?

HURT AND FEAR

My fear keeps me anchored
To a perpetual hurt.
Will logic give me impetus
To lift the anchor?

When I lack courage, I am immobilized, bitter
And envious of those who have the courage
To love, to separate, to grow.

If I am afraid of anger
Can I enjoy people?
If I am afraid of love
Can I enjoy sex?

If you are afraid of death,
Can you enjoy life?

RESISTANCE I

I'm afraid to learn
And I'm angry when I don't.

I'm afraid to leave
And I'm angry when I stay.

My mind goes round and round
With endless worry, remorse
And spineless adaptation.

What are you afraid to learn?
And what are you afraid to leave?

RESISTANCE II

Who you are intensifies
My dependent love.
What you do exacerbates
My earliest wounds.

Loving makes me too needy,
Too greedy, too angry,
Too frightened.
Loving makes me too crazy.

Is that really from my past?
Is that what you mean by transference?
And denial?
And resistance?

You are beginning to understand the concepts.
Recognizing your own overreaction
Is an important step in development.

CIRCULAR RUT

As I pursue my thoughts,
And reflect on my feelings,
I reach new depths
In my circular rut.

To break out of my rut
Takes the stoicism of a Spartan,
The imagination of an Athenian,
And the curiosity of a Biblical Scholar.

You have the imagination and curiosity.
Can you find the faith in yourself
To dig deeply enough
To recover the information you need
To climb out of your rut
And go on with your life?

I don't know yet.
But I think so.

ALTRUISM

I am "giving"
From a wealth of inner-tides:
Care, concern, fear, guilt, neediness
And some kind of learned ritual.

When you give up the ritual,
And separate
Care and concern
From
Fear, anger and neediness,
Then you won't give more
Than is comfortable
For your psyche
Or your soma.

SLEEPLESSNESS

When I can't sleep
I allow my images to come
And I explore them with diligence.

I cannot sleep when there is too much churning
Underneath the annoyances of the moment.
On the surface is too much suspicion.
I don't know yet what is underneath.

Whom do you suspect?
Of what?

DISTORTION AND SUSPICION

I could never be so mean to them,
And I couldn't believe they were so mean to me.
I invented a scenario
Where I was foolish and they were wise.
And that was the beginning of my myth.

Perhaps they weren't being mean.
Perhaps they were coping with their own problems.

That was where my suspicion began.
I suspected perhaps they were foolish,
And that made me foolish, too.

I pretended we were wise,
And I believed what I pretended.
But underneath, there lurked the fear
That I was only pretending.

And now?

I fool myself, I suspect myself, I catch myself,
Then I pay a penance.
I muddle my way through life.

As I learn to understand my early fears and myths,
I rearrange my clutter and reorganize my thoughts.

CHAPTER 3

SEEING CONNECTIONS

If you are willing to say your thoughts
Uncensored, as they come to mind
Together we will unravel the knots
That tie your past and present
Into an unseemly package.

SAFETY

This is a safe place for you
To say what you think you would like to say
To mother-father-grandparents-siblings-lovers-friends–
Self.
The words may come
From the tip of your tongue
Or the marrow of your bones.

FROM THE TIP OF MY TONGUE

I'm never going to speak to you again.
I'm going to tell you daily
That I'm never going to speak to you again.

And if you run away, I'll follow you
So I can continue to tell you that I am angry
Enough to never speak to you again.

THORN IN MY PSYCHE

I didn't trust them
But I did trust you.
When you became them
I couldn't trust you.

I didn't trust you
But I did trust me.
When I became you
I couldn't trust me.

I didn't trust me
But I did trust Him
When He became them
I couldn't trust Him.

Now I am trying
To learn once again
The basis of trust
And the nature of "them."

Feel trust sending out its sensors,
Feel your wounds healing,
Know that
Mistrust grows from festering wounds,
Healing wounds grow trust.

HUNGER AND LOVE

Sometimes it was me they loved.
Sometimes it was their own hunger
They were feeding.

That is a bitter bill to swallow,
And the pill does not relieve my pain.

If my pain is in my memory
Of their unsatisfied hunger,
How can I relieve my pain?

If you give to every hungry child you see,
Will that relieve the pain of memory?

No.

If you focus on your own hungers
Will that make life more palatable?

Not necessarily.

Can you know yourself, and feed yourself
And respect their hungers, too?

I don't know yet.

MASQUERADE

I don't want to hurt you
So I pretend pleasure.

I spend sleepless nights
Looking for ways
To feel passion
Dormant within.

I don't want to hurt you.
That's what this masquerade is about.

ASSAULT AND BATTERY

I won't believe you can't love me
And you won't believe that I don't hate you.
I meet your violence with my silence
As we act out our early fantasies.

Yours
Of revenge,

Mine
Of making peace.

I accept your apologies and tears of remorse
You accept my devotion.
We hope this time will be different.

It is really a team effort:
The battery provides the charge
To power the assault,
And the assault
Recharges the battery.
The battle is internal
As well as external.

FROM THE MARROW OF MY BONES

Fear is imbedded in my tissues.
Anger travels freely
Through the chambers of my heart.

I resurrect my fear
And redirect my anger
Over and over and over again.

ANATOMY IS DESTINY

We try to recapture our 3-year old rapture,
Our 2-year old mess interferes,
Our 2-year old tantrums leave us exhausted,
We regress to our pre-verbal blankets and tears.

The rapture, the mess, and the tiring tantrums,
The rhythms of hunger and cheer,
Remain in our tissues, our muscles, our posture,
Remain to remind us to lighten our cares.

Emotions are carried in anatomy.
Anatomy suggests limits and possibilities.
Possibilities and limits dynamically interact
With developing ego
To shape destiny.

CHAPTER 4

CHANGE

Indicating a readiness
To dig deeper.

HOVERCRAFT

Why do you hover between trust
And doubt?

Do you trust my knowledge
But doubt your ability
To give up drugs
Or the nipple
Or pain?

Why do you hover between concern
And attack?

Do you trust my concern
But doubt your ability
To give up obsessions
And compulsions?

Why do you hover between there
And here?

Do you doubt your ability
To develop your own
Identity?

TEMPERANCE

I let my temper flare
Or I swallow the fire.
The blazing rage is mine
As is the iciness of niceness.

I search through the embers that ignite.
I catch the winds that fan the heat.
I find distance and perspective
That allow me to discover
How to cool the coals
To a graying ash.

I quiet the rage that fuels my hate.

PEACE TREATIES

Shame, anger, fear, doubt,
Guilt and blind impatience,
Infiltrate my anatomy
In their feisty, foolish ways.

I listen thoughtfully,
Interpret cautiously,
Survive each conflict,

And use each truce to further look
For ways to establish a lasting peace.

LOOPHOLES

What kind of lies do I tell myself
About money and friendship
And caring and levity?

What kind of truths do I color and shade
About trust and love
And work and play?

When I uncover my lies and altered truths
I find my loopholes in my laws of gravity,
The ones through which I crawl
To save face and pacify my soul.

We use the lies to find the truth,
The kind of truth that heals the wounds
Found deep in the core of the psyche.

FRIENDSHIP

Strains In The Melody

First I say no,
Then you retaliate.

What starts as pleasant music
Becomes discordant sound.

The Duel

When I feel attacked by your defenses
And you feel engulfed by my inner needs
We thrust and we parry
And sidestep the issues
And try to relate as if all were well.

The Symphony

We learn to play together in harmony (but)
We know that dissonance may be good music (too).

LOST AND FOUND

Do I tame my libido
Or feign my libido,
Or give it full expression?

I lost my libido, I'm not sure when
It quietly slipped away.
My muse left also; they went underground
For an undetermined stay.

They romped and they played while incognito;
Then they returned to see
How the three of us could be together,
My muse, my libido, and me.

I LEARNED

First there was the chemistry
Of loving without understanding.

Then there was the chemistry
Of not wanting to understand,
Only wanting change.

Then there was the chemistry
Of loving and understanding
But having some doubt about my own direction.

The chemistry is all still there
But it no longer binds me
Or blinds me to my memories.

It no longer binds me to fantasy
Or blinds me to fact.

Charisma without depth is dangerous,
Data without imagery is dull,
Fact and fantasy intertwined
Tickle the fancy, shape the mind.

CORNERSTONES

Sharing is fun and is based on intimacy
Which is based on autonomy
Which is based on trust

Which is based on the pleasure of learning
To sit and stand and walk and talk
And use logic and emotions effectively

With those who understand
The language of their bodies
As well as the language of their souls

ON BEING STUBBORN

BOOK II

BEYOND THE CONSCIOUS

BENEATH THE SYMPTOMS

RETRIEVAL

When knowledge from the psyche
Comes clearly into view,
Middle age is extended and old age is available
To be valued and enjoyed
Until death.

Look inside yourself to discover your own metaphors,
Your pictograms of infancy, your hieroglyphs of youth.
Then translate your personal Rosetta Stone.

STRUCTURAL CHANGE

The symptoms of emotional distress are like icebergs; the tips that show are a small part of the vast emotional structure that is an important part of the framework on which we build our lives. In our search to find what lies beneath obvious symptoms we discover our early conflicts and new ways to resolve them. We also discover the accuracy and inaccuracy of early learning.

There is a wide chasm between identifying symptoms and understanding the structure beneath them. There is an even wider chasm between understanding the structure and developing the tools to change one's own attitudes and behaviors.

Recognizing symptoms has brought us to therapy. Developing the therapeutic alliance and seeing connections between current feelings and early myths and fears began the therapeutic work. Using images, dreams, logic, and impulse control, to change one's own emotional structure is what this step of the work is about.

Allow your imagination to leap and trust your therapist to help you define your boundaries.

CHAPTER I

FROM THE PSYCHE

Thoughts unfolding tell me my secrets
Each image brings forth another truth.

MEDITATION

I see with my inner eye,
I sense with my inner Self.
I gradually recover information
That is stored in my nooks and crannies.

I discover the origins
Of my buried thorns
And my many-pronged horns.

I discover rage
In the muscles of my jaw,

I locate fear
In my solar plexus,

I find spite and grudge
In unlikely places,

And uncover my wisdom,
My humor,
My love.

EARLY INJURIES

When I find the troubled places
And try to clean the wounds,
I am face to face with how much I need
What they were unable to give.
I am face to face with how much I want
What I still have not achieved.

When I salve my wounds with fantasy
I feel a temporary relief.
My depression lifts;
My anxiety lessens;
And I experience my world
With a temporary delight.

Some hurts need to be softened
And dissolved.
There is no other way to heal.

RESONANCE

Sometimes my lips say it,
But I don't feel it in my bones.

Sometimes I feel it in my bones
But I can't get the words past my throat.

If I force the words past my throat
I say them too fast, or so quietly
I barely hear myself.

My stomach, my glands, and my muscles
Sometimes harmonize, sometimes are dissonant.

When they are dissonant,
I learn something new.
When they harmonize,
My words come from a place
Deep inside my being.

HANDS

Where are the hands,
The warm hands, the kind hands,
The musical hands, the magical hands,
The calloused hands, the competent hands,
Where are the hands, the gentle generous hands
That steadied my world when I was a child?

CHAPTER 2

AND SO WE GO DEEPER

For some the trauma began before birth,
For some it began at the breast.
Where did it strike? Where did it rest?

BLOWS TO THE PSYCHE

For some the trauma began with speech,
For others with touch or with time.
Were the shocks crippling? Were they benign?

The psyche sustains both pleasure and pain
That filter into memory and filter out again
Through many distorting lenses.

Love and hunger,
Fear and anger,
Guilt and shame.
All combine
To blur and twist
Our very early memories.

THE PSYCHOANALYTIC MICROSCOPE

We look at each piece of memory
Through the objective lenses
Of experience, knowledge, and compassion
Which allow us to view
The messages in our dreams,
And the metaphors of our lives
With clarity and light.

A DREAM

When my mother was twenty-five
Her baby was not quite two.
I was a tiny foetus
Preparing myself for birth.

My first consciousness
Was her heart-beat
Strong and steady.

Then I heard the roar
And rumble of blood
As it carried food
To every cell in our bodies.

I heard the grumble of her gut
As she complained about our burdens.
I felt the tingle of hormones
As they tickled my toes.

I sailed the waters of my world,
My uterine world of the distant past,
And there I enjoyed a dimension of bliss.

A DREAM CONTINUED

In her womb I felt the oneness,
The wonder, the awe.
In the warmth and floating darkness
I knew trust.

I carry the memory
Of senses awakening
Of muscles flexing.

I carry the memory
Of the steady pressure
That propelled me into birth.

I carry the memory
Of emerging
From darkness into light.

My birth was more traumatic
For my mother than for me,
And I quickly learned the pleasures of my mouth,
Just as I had once known the pleasures of her womb.

The pleasures in my mouth
Were interrupted by the pain of teething.
I thought my misery would never lighten,
But it did.

Softness of skin and sweetness of breast
Relieved some of the pain of growing.
Firm loving hands nurtured my growth
And I thrived with the pleasure of learning.

BIRTH

It came as no surprise
That in my mother's eyes
I was beautiful
But not yet very wise.

Do you trust what you saw
In Mother's eyes?

ALL SYSTEMS GO

I gave them information
With my respiration
Circulation,
Digestion,
Bladder, bowels,
Skin and muscles.

I spoke to them with my eyes and my lips.

When they read me correctly, I trusted us all.
On that trust, I based my later learning.

When they didn't understand my language
I tried to learn theirs.

We became friends
Despite the language difficulty.

THEM

I imagined her to be
The most wonderful human
It was possible to be.

I imagined him to be
Even more than she.

So you started life seeking perfection
Instead of being satisfied
With excellent, very good,
Or good enough.

ON BEING STUBBORN

When my parents had another child
I told myself I'd never speak again.
I kept the things they gave me,
The useful and the useless,
I loved them very much,
But I didn't speak
For many years
On matters
Important.

You are speaking of important matters now!

DILEMMA

When I stay in this spot in relation to them,
I distort, complain, obsess, and suffer.
When I take a step or two away,
I somehow see more clearly
My own shape and my own
Direction.

What does it mean to you when you say,
"I'll take a step or two away"?

SEPARATION AND CONNECTION

At first I was furious.
I stayed to fight it out.

Then I was hurt and disappointed.
I cried.
I licked my wounds.

I took some little steps
Into a larger world
Where I didn't lean.

The stronger I grew
The more appreciative I was
For all I had learned while leaning.

WALLS

I put up some walls
Many years ago
To protect me from invasion.
The stones are weathered
And covered with ivy

And attractive in their way.

Are your walls boundaries or barriers?

Sometimes my walls are boundaries that define me.
Sometimes my walls are barriers that exclude you.

Who is "you"?

I don't know yet . . . .

Can you repair walls that were built on faults?

PASSAGES

I dreamed of unsound bridges,
Darkened tunnels, endless stairways,
And icy roads.

I dreamed of mountain wild-flowers,
Modern buildings, centaurs,
And Camelot.

Your dreams are an entry to your inner world.
The bridges you build represent your transitions.
The tunnels you dig are your underground feelings.

Crawl carefully through your darkened tunnels,
Creep thoughtfully across your faulty bridges.
Build your stairways to somewhere
And thaw your icy roads.

Scale your walls,
Relight your tunnels,
Rebuild your bridges

Then enjoy the mountains and the myths
And the architecture of your choice.

TRANSITION

I was angry, frightened
And hungry for something.

I overslept, I overate,
I overworked, I overplayed,
I overpouted, I overspent,
I overdid a lot of things
Because I was hungry for something,
I didn't yet know what.

And then I crossed a bridge.

IMAGES

I chip away at the walls
That have outlived their usefulness.
They are structures that began to form
When I was too tender to cope with my realities.
Today they prevent me from realizing my life.

I created myths to explain incomprehensible data.
My myths made my infant and child worlds
More palatable, but they wreak havoc
With my life today.

This wall is gray, made of heavy stones.
It is covered with ivy that is intensely green.
The stones are deceptively smooth, and uniform.
The wall effectively narrows my world.

This wall surrounds my castle
Whose safety I reinforce with a moat
In which I keep crocodiles who eat
Anyone who tries to Know me.

This wall is a barbed wire
That keeps you at a distance
Even when I want you close.

This wall is a picket fence
Surrounding my garden and house.
My garden is full of colorful flowers,
Nutritious vegetables and fragrant herbs.
There are no weeds in my garden.
My house is never untidy.

I put up the walls when I needed them.
I find it difficult to take them down.

CROSSING BRIDGES

To make the transition
From good little child
To teasing adolescent,
The good little child
Needs to feel "good"
About sexual appetites.

To make the transition
From teasing adolescent
To loving adult,
The teasing adolescent
Needs to understand
Anxiety beneath defenses.

WISHES AND FEARS, RESOLVING

In the beginning
They listened to what I had to say.
For reasons I know now
They went away.

So I learned to listen to myself.

In the beginning
They saw me as I was.
For reasons I know now
Their vision clouded.

So I learned to see myself.

In the beginning
I was the center of their universe.
For reasons I know now
Their interests broadened.

So I developed a center of my own.

I moved to their periphery,
I orbited around them
Until I developed my own interests
And enough energy to leave their system

And developed a life of my own.

When I realize my part in the deception . . .

BOOK III

FINISHING TOUCHES

THE GRAPH OF LIFE

It is easier to approach emotional problems
With the healthy energy
Of knowledge
Instead of attacking them
With the shallow energy
Of blame and spite
When we know with certainty
That life is unfair.

Weltschmerz
And joi-de-vivre
Are the X and Y of reality.

The Z remains to be defined.

BEYOND THERAPY

Infant and childhood experiences endure in the long term memory and have unlimited possibilities of expression in adult life. We create our own universes and build our own prisons within the reality of our genetic roots and the learning that takes place before we have language or logical thought.

Early environment includes the emotional health and ill-health of nuclear and extended families as well as that of the social, political and economic structure of the larger world. As we respond to the complexity of life we learn to love people who are considerably less than perfect and whose demands are sometimes considerably greater than we can meet.

In psychotherapy we learn to go beyond self-deception and trivia. The early learning that is intricately and delicately woven into our lives is carefully and thoughtfully explored from many angles and planes. The careful, thoughtful exploration leads to inner healing that opens us to dimensions of living that are not strangled by *our own* obsessive compulsive hysteric borderline nonsense.

During the learning process, we recognize discomfort before it takes us over the edge. We develop a deeper understanding of cause and effect. And we have more compassion for those who know not what they do, because we have more skill in protecting ourselves from *their* obsessive compulsive hysteric borderline nonsense.

Beyond therapy, this is a life-long process.

CHAPTER I

PATTERNS

When I look, what do I see?
Was it them?
Or is it me?
Am I a puppet up my ancestral tree?

FAMILY SYSTEMS

They were addictive or compulsive
And sometimes some of both.

They were frantic or immobilized
And somewhere in between.

From generation to generation
The senses through which the world was perceived
Were blurred and distorted.

We find a way to correct the distortions,
Clear the senses,
And learn.

MORTALITY

On any family tree
Some of the branches are dead wood
While other branches grow.

But even the dead wood is part of the tree
And we all feel like dead wood sometimes.

We all sometimes wake up in the night, angry.
And daytimes we try to let go of the anger.
All trees eventually have
Withered leaves,
Dead branches,
Dying roots.

They all become part of the compost
That feeds the saplings.

ACCOMODATION

I told you what I didn't like.
When you didn't understand,
I was angry.

When you offered me a pacifier,
My anger ebbed.

Who is "you?"

FRUSTRATION

You made a mistake.
You made a mistake.
And I told you about it.
Now you are compounding it.
Why do you compound the mistake
After I clearly tell you how I feel?

I bang my head against your walls
And the rhythm of the banging
Relieves the terror that I feel.

Who is "you?"

RAGE

I was so angry I wanted to die.
Then I was frightened, and started to cry.
Then, I plotted and planned my revenge.
I would live long, and grow strong enough
To control you.

And that gave my life purpose.

Who is "you?"

DEPRESSION

I keep running away from my anger.
It is easier to carry the smoldering rage
In the form of grudge
And spite
And irritation
Than to allow my spine to relax
Into its natural shape.

TRAGEDY

She sacrificed her life at the alter
Of some being she had created
In her imagination.

He sacrificed his life
At the altar of her needs.

Can I learn to live my life
Without feeling like a sacrificial lamb?

SELF-CENTERED LOVE

When you did not learn
To live comfortably
In my world,
I did not wish you well.

Who is "you?"

DEPENDENT LOVE

We blurred our emotional boundaries;
I blamed me when you had a headache,
And you blamed you when I reached exhaustion

We embraced each other in a pool
In which we both nearly drowned.

PARENTAL LOVE

It was their land
And they shared it with me.
It was no reflection on their ancestors
Or progeny.
They shared their love of their country with me,
A stranger.

CHAPTER 2

THE FAMILY SYMPTOMS

The rigid structure tumbles
And crumbles into dust
As I explore my meanings of
I can
I shall
I may, I might
I will, I won't
I must!

NARCISSISM

I sucked them in
I sucked them dry
And that's what made them
Bitter.

They sucked me in
They sucked me dry
So I am bitter,
Too.

The milk that once was sweet
Turned sour.
The aftertaste
Is Bitter.

What passed for love
Has turned to rage.
Was it merely hunger pangs?

ADDICTION

I mistook my hunger for love
And overlooked my anger.
I was so intent on pleasing them
I scarcely noticed myself.

I neglected myself,
Then I overdosed
To get my attention.

RIGHTEOUSNESS

If drugs make me feel good
What can be wrong with them?

If overwork feels industrious
What can be wrong with it?

If casual sex is exciting
What can be wrong with it?

If killing achieves stability
What can be wrong with it?

REPRESSION

I am tired of being controlled
By feelings that are connected to events
That lie just beyond my available memory.

When did I begin to thwart myself?
Was it when I was nursing at mother's breast,
Or sitting on father's knee, playing with his ears
And tugging at his beard, and loving the smell of him?

Did I add him to the world I had shared with her,
Or did I banish her to make room for him?
Did I have to vie with too many others
For a special look or touch?

Am I afraid or ashamed or too angry
To remember how much I loved
The feel and sound and look
And touch and smell
Of them?

LOGIC

I wasn't the cause of his depression,
But was he the cause of my rage?

(What is the cause of his depression and my rage?)

I wasn't the cause of her anxiety
But was she the cause of mine?

(What is the cause of my anxiety?)

DECEPTION

When I feel like a deceived small child,
I am frightened, enraged, and uncertain
Of my boundaries.

When I realize my part in the deception,
I am rueful, chagrined, and I try not to be at odds
With myself.

CHAPTER 3

INNER LANDSCAPE OUTER WORLD

Explore until you are able
To see the inner and the outer
Without distorting the details.

PROEM

In the beginning it seems so easy.
We breathe, we eat, we smile, we sleep.
We digest our food and eliminate the waste.
We coo, we cry, we crawl, we walk,
And trust the people we please.

We talk and play and read and write
And we ready ourselves for living life.
Some learn to balance books,
Some learn to balance equations,
And some understand
$E = mc^2$

We also learn to twist logic,
Distort facts,
And deny reality,
As we try to make sense
Of our own humanity
And inhumanity.

If we survived the mistakes that others made,
We thrive as we discover our own!

THE CHILD'S FEAR

As a child I lay awake many nights
Frightened of ogres and beasts.
My imagery was of war, of men killing men,
And doing something odious to women.
I didn't know what.

I knew that men were often unkind and powerful.
I didn't know that yet about women.

I knew that women were often gentle and kind.
I didn't know that yet about men.

ADULT ANXIETY

I'm having a very bad dream,
And I am terrified.
I'm terrified of a mentality
I find everywhere.

I hear it in the threats and counter-threats
Of political rhetoric.
I taste it in the poisoned food-chain,
I breathe it in the polluted air,
I sense it in the haters
Who rape and mug.

I see it in the corporate leaders who have
More concern for the balance sheet
Than for balanced people.

I feel it in the bullies who massacre
Under the guise of "teaching a lesson."

I am terrified of a mentality
That I find everywhere,
Even in me.

EXISTENTIAL

I speculate my future,
I investigate my past,
I live in the present.

I dream about the future,
I dream about the past,
I live in the present.

There seems to be no limit
To the depth of knowledge,
But my depth of despair
Tapers off.

What can be worse than genocide
Or earthquakes
Or child abuse
Or prejudice
Or tidal waves
Or jealousy
Or terror of God's wrath?

EXCESSES

Anger focuses vision;
Rage obscures it.

Hunger sharpens perceptions;
Starvation distorts them.

Fear teaches caution;
Terror imprisons.

Trust teaches love;
Dependence is blinding.

There is nothing to be learned from prolonged excess,
Nor of prolonged poverty of any kind.

RECOVERY

They taught me respect.
And I learned
To protect my autonomy.

They taught me to read the clock.
And I learned
To manage time.

They taught me
Grassy meadows, haystacks, pussy willows, lakes,
Cold mountain air, music, colors,
And much much more.

And I learned to love learning.

PAPA FREUD

He shared his shame,
Explored his guilt,
Revealed his rage,
And showed us how he used his tools
So we could learn to use our own.

With courage and wisdom
He showed us love.

EPILOGUE

Kindred souls in parallel planes
Travel together for a period in time.
When we leave to go our separate ways
Each is richer for the experience.

COLOPHON

LEAPS AND BOUNDARIES *was designed by Linnea Lundquist and printed by Sequoyah Graphics. The typefaces are Trump Mediaeval and Codex, both designed by Georg Trump.*